MY
NAME
IS
Bana

To all the children who were
scattered in refugee camps and
who were separated from their
parents because of war
—B. A.

To my Teta and Jiddo
—N. R.

SALAAM
READS

An imprint of Simon & Schuster Children's Publishing Division
1230 Avenue of the Americas, New York, New York 10020
Text © 2021 by Bana Alabed
Illustration © 2021 by Nez Riaz
Book design by Lucy Ruth Cummins © 2021 by Simon & Schuster, Inc.
For information about special discounts for bulk purchases, please contact Simon & Schuster
Special Sales at 1-866-506-1949 or business@simonandschuster.com.
The Simon & Schuster Speakers Bureau can bring authors to your live event. For more information
or to book an event, contact the Simon & Schuster Speakers Bureau at 1-866-248-3049 or
visit our website at www.simonspeakers.com.
The text for this book was set in Aunt Mildred.
The illustrations for this book were rendered in acrylic paint and finished in Procreate.
Manufactured in China
0621 SCP
First Edition
2 4 6 8 10 9 7 5 3 1
Library of Congress Cataloging-in-Publication Data
Names: Alabed, Bana, 2009– author. | Riaz, Nez, illustrator.
Title: My name is Bana / Bana Alabed ; illustrated by Nez Riaz.
Description: First edition. | New York : Salaam Reads, 2021. | Audience:
Ages 4–8. | Audience: Grades K–1. | Summary: Bana's mother tells her of the strong bana tree that
grows in their homeland, Syria, and how Bana's strength helped her survive war, being a refugee,
and starting fresh in a new country.
Identifiers: LCCN 2020055974 |
ISBN 9781534412484 (hardcover) | ISBN 9781534412507 (ebook)
Subjects: LCSH: Alabed, Bana, 2009–—Juvenile literature. | Refugee children—United States—
Biography—Juvenile literature. | Syria—History—Civil War, 2011-—Personal narratives—Juvenile
literature. | Syrian Americans—Biography—Juvenile literature. | Children's writings, American.
Classification: LCC DS98.72.A36 A3 2021 | DDC 956.9104/231092—dc23
LC record available at https://lccn.loc.gov/2020055974

# MY NAME IS Bana

words by **BANA ALABED**
pictures by **NEZ RIAZ**

**SALAAM**
READS

**New York London Toronto Sydney New Delhi**

"Why did you name me Bana?"

I ask my mother one day.

She tells me that I am named after a tall bushy tree
that grows in Syria, the country where I was born.
"It is my favorite," she says. She shows me a picture of
a tree with light green leaves that rise to the sky.

"Your baba and I wanted you to always be *qawia* just like this tree."

Momma speaks to me
in Arabic, the language
of the country where
I was born. I know
that *qawia* means
"strong" in English,
because I speak that
language too.

"But what does it mean to be strong, Momma?"

"It means . . .

that you are brave even when you are scared."

"It means that you always help other people—you are sturdy so they can lean on you."

"It means you use your mighty voice to speak up when you see something that is wrong or unfair."

"It means you study and read lots of books
so your mind will be powerful."

"It means that you run and jump and exercise so your body will be fit."

"Am I strong?"
I ask Momma.

I think I am but
I want to be sure.

"Oh yes, my Bon Bon, you are very strong,"
Momma tells me, and she gives me that look where
I can see the love shining in her eyes.

It was good that Momma and Baba gave me this very special name because when war came to my country, I had to be strong,

just like the tree. . . .

When bombs fell from the sky, I had to be very brave even though it was loud and scary and we always had to hide.

When my little brothers were sad and scared, I had to comfort them and take care of them.

One time, I built a playground in the living room when we couldn't go outside because of the war. Momma said it was very clever.

When I flew on an airplane to a country I had never been to,

I had to learn many new things and make all new friends.

When I decided to tell the whole world what was going on in my country, I traveled to many different places to give speeches to adults to remind them that all children should be safe, and have food to eat, clean water, and a good education.

"Is that how I am strong like the tree?" I ask Momma.

"Yes, my love."

"Even when I was scared, or sad, or I missed my family, and I always told myself that it would be better soon?"

"Yes!" she says.

"That is also what it means to be strong.
Maybe the most important part.
To always have *amal*."

I know what *amal*
means in English.

It is ... "hope."

"You will always be strong and you will always have hope, right, little one?"

Momma gives me that hug that makes all my insides mush together. My favorite kind.

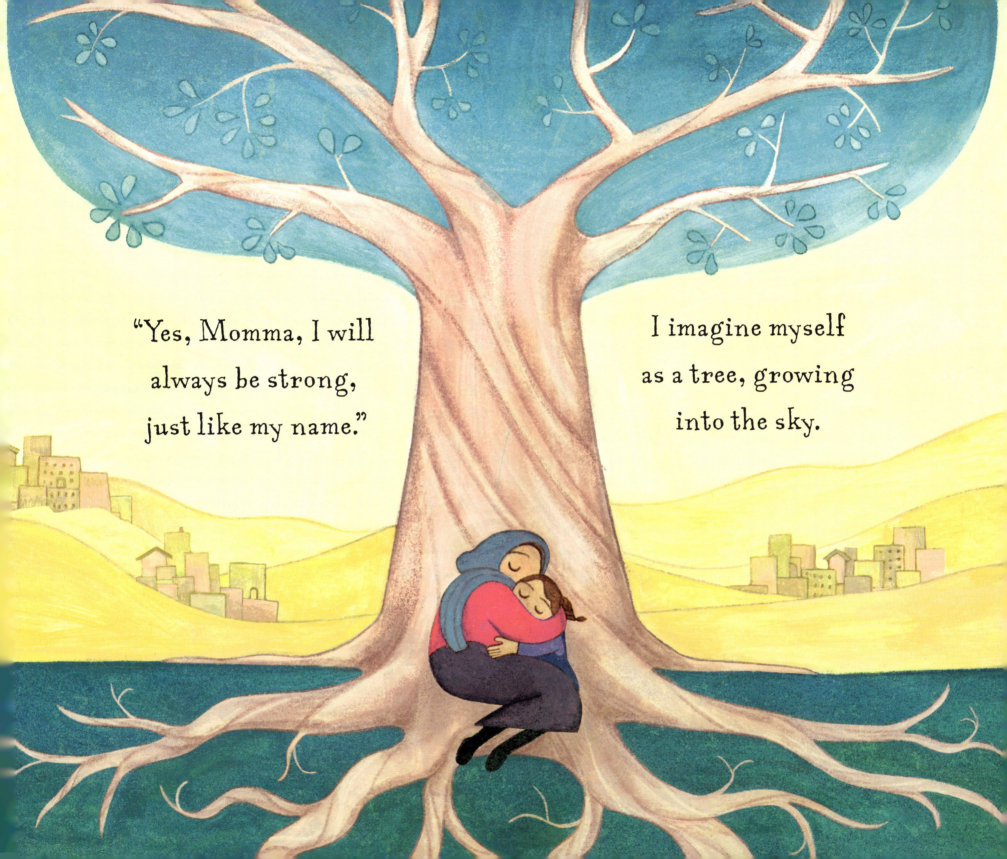

"Yes, Momma, I will always be strong, just like my name."

I imagine myself as a tree, growing into the sky.

I am **so** strong.

My brothers' names are Lieth and Noor. They are named for a lion and light.

Those are good
names too:
lions are
powerful and
light is good.

But I would rather be a tree.

# AUTHOR'S NOTE

**I am safe now.** I live in Turkey with my parents and two little brothers and I get to go to school every day, for the first time in my life. I love everything about my school and getting to learn and be clever, but my favorite subjects are math and reading.

For a long time, I didn't get to go to school and I was not safe. War broke out in my country when I was very small. Before that, my dad was a lawyer and my mom was in school to become a lawyer too, and I lived near all my many aunts, uncles, cousins, and grandparents—all of my family had lived in Syria forever and ever.

As soon as the bombs started to fall, everything changed. My mom and dad couldn't work anymore, and my school was blown up. It was often too dangerous to even leave the house, and many times we had to run and hide in the dark basement when we heard the loud *vroom* of the planes coming. And it just got worse and worse. My best friend, Yasmin, was killed, and my house was destroyed. My family and I had to live on the streets of Aleppo with little food or water or medicine. We didn't know if we would live or die.

One day, I asked my mom if people in the world knew what was happening to us. I wanted someone to help us—that is why I went on Twitter, so I could ask people to help to bring peace to my country. That was my first tweet—"I NEED PEACE." I made a hashtag called #standwithaleppo.

People from all over the world saw my tweets. They sent nice messages and reporters, and leaders in other countries began to pay attention to what was happening to innocent people. When people listened, it gave me hope. I just had to be strong.

Finally, my family got to be evacuated to Turkey. Our escape took a long time and was very scary. And then we became refugees. We were happy to be safe from the bombs, but it is hard to live in a place where you don't know anyone or speak the language or know much about the culture. But I love to learn languages and meet new people, so it's a fun adventure too.

Ever since we escaped, I have traveled to different places—to England, to America, to Germany—to tell people my story of surviving a war and ask people to help other kids around the world, thousands of them, who are still living in war zones. Who don't have access to clean water and medicine. Who can't go to school and learn.

That is why I wanted to write this book—for them. So I can tell them: **be strong.**

But I have a message for adults, too: **Kids shouldn't have to always be so strong. Every child deserves to live in peace.**